5-Minute Devotional Tune-Ups:

Daily Psalms for Spiritual Renewal

Dr. Raymond Grabert, Jr.

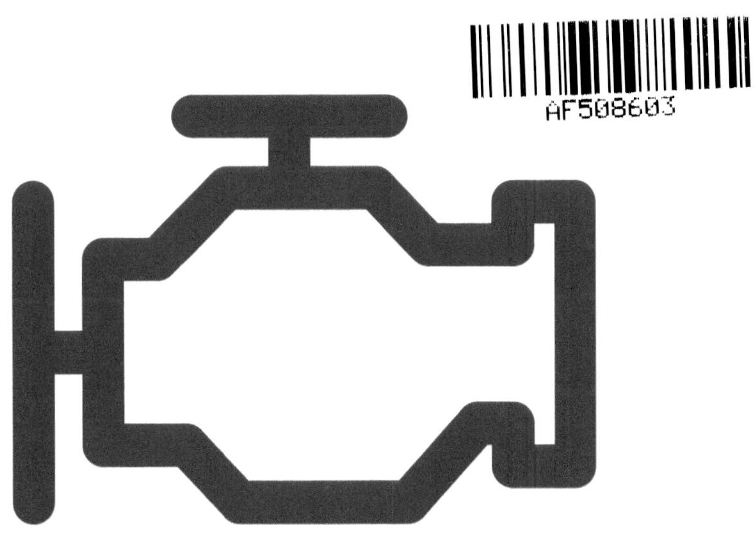

A Devotional from the series:
"Coffee With The Preacher"

ISBN 979-8-89965-905-8
Printed in the United States of America.
For information, contact: Dr. Raymond Grabert, 3211 Big Ridge Rd,
Diberville, MS 39540

To you who desire to know God
more-- May this devotional encourage
you to draw closer to Him!

May the Psalms deepen and awaken
your soul to His presence.

As you sit with a warm cup of coffee
in hand, may you find the comfort of
the Holy Spirit as you experience a
"Tune-Up" from His Word!

ALL FOR CHRIST!

Dr. Raymond GRABERT

Table Of Contents

Notes

Introduction

Before You Begin

Devotions

Closing Remarks

Author Bio

Notes

Scripture quotations have been taken from the Christian Standard Bible®, Copyright © 2017 by Holman Bible Publishers. Used by permission. Christian Standard Bible® and CSB® are federally registered trademarks of Holman Bible Publishers.

This manuscript was proofread and edited with the assistance of Chatgpt to identify grammatical errors, improve clarity, and ensure consistency. The manuscript was then proofread by Wanda Bowman for further identification of grammatical errors. All suggested edits were reviewed and finalized by the author, who remains responsible for the final content.

Introduction

Automobiles have always been a big part of my life. I grew up in a family where my grandfather was a mechanic for a Dodge dealer in Thibodaux, Louisiana. My father, though not working in the automobile industry, was a shade-tree mechanic. Dad and his friends were always tinkering and fixing their cars when something broke. I spent a lot of time with them repairing broken parts, and have a love for turning wrenches whenever I can. This devotional, like my previous three, takes my love for God's Word and blends it with one of my earthly loves. Tune-ups are a necessity if your car or truck is to run its best. Our hearts also need the fine adjustment from the Holy Spirit to keep our lives on track with our Heavenly Father. The Book of Psalms is a great resource to stir us to make needed repairs and adjustments. Join me in taking 5 minutes at a time to "Tune-Up" our hearts. We will invest in short reflections, Bible-based questions, and practical advice to help us maintain our hearts.

ALL FOR CHRIST!

Dr. Raymond GRABERT

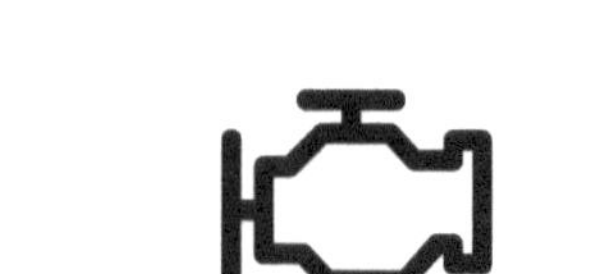

Before You Begin

1. God's Word is most important! My words are just that, my words. Scripture always is first in our lives.

2. Take your time. Do not rush the process! Read and reread God's Word. Allow it to saturate your heart and mind.

3. Remember, my words are just that, my words. These are my heart expressions when I read and meditated on God's Word.

4. Reflect along the way. Each devotion comes with questions to guide your thoughts and apply that passage to your life.

5. The Gospel of Jesus Christ is our foundation.
   - We are sinners under the condemnation of God's judgment. Romans 3:23
   - Jesus gave His life to pay our sin debt. Romans 5:8
   - God, through the sacrifice of Jesus, has given us life as a free gift. Romans 6:23
   - We receive salvation when we place our faith and trust in the work of Jesus Christ on the cross on our behalf. Romans 10:13

Tune-Up 1

Psalm 1:2 - Instead, his delight is in the Lord's instruction, and he meditates on it day and night.

A good tune-up always starts with having the right tools ready to address any issues. Along with the right tools comes the awareness that something may be out of adjustment. The psalmist reminds us that the person who makes God's Word his standard has the greatest potential for right living. Just as a tune-up keeps a car running according to the manufacturer's design, meditating on Scripture keeps our lives aligned with God's purpose. When we delight in His Word day and night, we notice when something in us is off balance. The Holy Spirit then works to renew our hearts and minds, bringing us back into alignment with His will. A true disciple finds joy in this process, knowing that God's Word is the standard by which we live and the source that keeps our lives running strong.

In The Garage

Read and meditate on Psalm 1 each morning this week.

1. In what areas of life do you sense a feeling of being "out of tune" with God's Word, and what Scriptures could help realign your heart and actions?

2. How can you make meditating on Scripture a more consistent part of your daily routine so that you stay spiritually "tuned up"?

3. How do you respond when the Holy Spirit reveals something in you that needs adjustment? What would it look like to welcome His correction as part of your growing as a disciple?

He is like a tree planted beside flowing streams that bears its fruit in its season and whose leaf does not wither. Whatever he does prospers.
Psalm 1:3

Tune-Up 2

Psalm 16:8 - I always let the Lord guide me. Because He is at my right hand, I will not be shaken.

Our feeling of security and stability is only as strong as the foundation beneath it. The psalmist had placed his faith fully in God, and as a result, he experienced a deep sense of safety in the presence of the Lord. It's a lot like caring for our car. When our maintenance is regular, we have confidence in its ability to carry us wherever we need to go. In the same way, when our faith is well-maintained, when our trust and focus are centered on God, we can move through life with assurance. God steadies our hearts and stabilizes our steps so that we can, like the psalmist, boldly declare, "I will not be shaken." This kind of confidence doesn't come from ourselves or our circumstances. It comes only when our footing is firm in God. Our gaze is fixed on Him. Our hearts are set on the One who can carry us through both the good and the difficult times. So where is your heart's gaze today? Is your life aligned with God's Word and His ways? Let's keep our trust tuned to the One who never fails, and rest secure in His unshakable presence.

In The Garage

Begin each day by praying for God to guide your focus.

1. What are you relying on for security? Have you placed trust in things that can shift or fail?

2. What are the daily practices that help maintain your "spiritual life" the way you would maintain your car?

3. What steps can you take to look to Him quickly and confidently?

Lord, You are my portion and my cup of blessing;
You hold my future.
Psalm 16:5

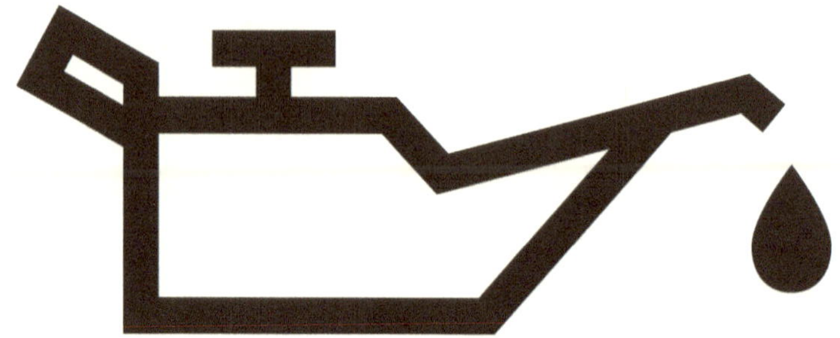

This light is a warning that your engine oil is low. Low oil leads to low lubrication in your engine. If left unattended, catastrophe lies ahead.

Low Oil Light

Psalm 23:5 — You prepare a table before me in the presence of my enemies; you anoint my head with oil; my cup overflows.

Tune-Up 3

Psalm 18:2 - The Lord is my rock, my fortress, and my deliverer, my God , my rock where I seek refuge, my shield and the horn of my salvation, my stronghold.

Car repairs can be very stressful. With the complexity of modern automobiles, a skilled mechanic can be hard to find. We look for a shop we can trust, and once we find one, we become return customers. We listen to their advice because we know they have the knowledge and experience to help us keep things running smoothly. Spiritually, we should follow the words of the psalmist. God has proven Himself faithful time and again. He is our rock, our fortress, and our deliverer. Even in the most difficult circumstances we face, God walks with us and guides us through. When we place our trust in Him, an inner strength begins to develop. We can live with confidence in His love and care for us. Through His Word, He gives us the guidance we need, and as we listen, we begin to make the necessary adjustments in our lives, just as we would follow a trusted mechanic's advice for required repairs on our car or truck. God can be trusted to show us what needs attention and to help us make those much-needed repairs in our hearts and habits. So in every challenge, lean on His strength rather than your own. He knows exactly what's needed to keep your life running in the right direction.

In The Garage

Write down one area where you need to rely on God's power this week.

1. Where do you need to "trust the Master Mechanic" instead of trying to fix things alone?

2. What specific area is God revealing that needs attention or repair, and how can you respond to allow Him to start repairs?

3. How has God already proven Himself faithful as my rock, fortress, and deliverer, and how can remembering that build your trust today?

God — His way is perfect, the word of the Lord is pure. He is a shield to all who take refuge in Him.
Psalm 18:30

Tune-Up 4

Psalm 19:14 -May the words of my mouth and the meditation of my heart be acceptable to You, Lord, my rock and my Redeemer.

The psalmist understood the relationship between the heart and the mouth. The focus of the heart is revealed by the words of the mouth. The two are so closely connected that the by-product of their relationship is unmistakable. When the heart is set on God, the words spoken are righteous, lovely, pure, and holy. God is pleased with such words because the heart behind them is the same. The exhaust of a car's engine reveals much about its inner condition. As leaky valves, worn rings, or an improper fuel mixture show themselves in the exhaust, our words reveal the state of our hearts. If the words we speak are unholy, harsh, or mean, it is a sign that our hearts are not aligned with God and His ways. We can evaluate our spiritual condition by listening to the words we speak to or about others. Steps can then be taken to bring the heart into step with the Holy Spirit. When the heart is aligned with Him, the words that flow from it, and the meditations behind them, become acceptable and pleasing to our God.

In The Garage

Pause to briefly pray before speaking in difficult moments.

1. What recent words from your mouth reveal about the current state of your heart before God?

2. Where is your speech drifting toward harshness, complaint, or impurity, and what might the Holy Spirit be inviting you to address within?

3. What step or steps can you take this week to align your heart more closely with God so that spoken words become a reflection of His character?

The precepts of the Lord are right, making the heart glad; the command of the Lord is radiant, making the eyes light up.
Psalm 19:8

The traction control system, abbreviated "TC" or "TCS," is an active safety feature that helps to keep a car's grip between the tires and the road in slippery or dangerous conditions.

Traction Control Light

Psalm 66:9 — He keeps us alive and does not allow our feet to slip.

Tune-Up 5

Psalm 23:1 - The Lord is my shepherd; I have what I need.

"Trust" is a word that seems to get tossed around today with little real meaning behind it. Yet trust affects not only the small matters of life but the important ones as well. Choosing which mechanic to take our car to is one such important matter. We have to trust them to diagnose and fix what is wrong. And we also hope that our mechanic won't take advantage of that trust. Another serious area of our lives that involves trust? Our spiritual lives. Just like our cars, we experience problems and need repairs. We all look for someone who can give us solid, dependable advice. So the question becomes: Who do you trust to guide your life? Psalm 23 reminds us that we can trust God. David declared that the Lord was his shepherd. He had learned to trust the hand of God at work in his life. Knowing God would provide, guide, and protect him, he willingly trusted that no matter what happened, God could be counted on. Our Lord provides everything we need. As you trust your mechanic with what you can't fix on your own, trust God with the things you cannot repair in your heart and life. Rest in His care and His provision. And remember, the greatest provision He has given us is salvation through His Son, Jesus Christ. Need repairs? Trust in God.

In The Garage

List three areas where God has provided for you lately.

1. Where in your life are you struggling to trust God's guidance, and what would it look like to place that "repair" in His hands today?

2. Consider the three areas where God provided, protected, or guided recently, and how can remembering these moments strengthen your trust in Him now?

3. What voices or "advisors" are you turning to for life direction, and how can you make God's Word your primary source of guidance?

He renews my life; he leads me along the right paths
for his name's sake.
Psalm 23:3

Tune-Up 6

Maintaining a car or truck is more than turning a wrench or twisting a screwdriver. You need the right knowledge to go with those actions. Knowing which bolt to loosen, how tight to tighten it, and which part to address is vital to keeping a vehicle running well. Maintaining our spiritual lives is much the same. It's more than praying, reading, and meditating. We must know what to pray, what to read, and what to meditate on. A well-guided disciple knows God's commands and His gentle admonitions. Bible study becomes a kind of spiritual repair manual. As a manual guides us to diagnose and fix broken parts, Scripture reveals what is broken within us and directs us toward the repair our hearts desperately need. All of this is done through the power of the Holy Spirit as we grow in the knowledge of God's Word. Like the psalmist in Psalm 25, we cry out for the Lord to make His ways known to us. When we desire to be guided by His truth, His commands, and His mercy, we place ourselves in the best position to have a properly ordered, well-guided, and faithfully operating life in Christ.

In The Garage

Meditate on Psalm 25:4-5 at the start of each day this week.

1. Where do you sense "broken parts" that God's Word has revealed, and are you willing to let the Holy Spirit guide the repairs?

2. How intentional are you about knowing what to pray, read, and meditate on, rather than simply going through spiritual routines?

3. In what ways can you allow the cry of Psalm 25 to teach God's ways and guide you into a more ordered, Christ-centered life?

The Lord is good and upright; therefore, he shows sinners the way.
Psalm 25:9

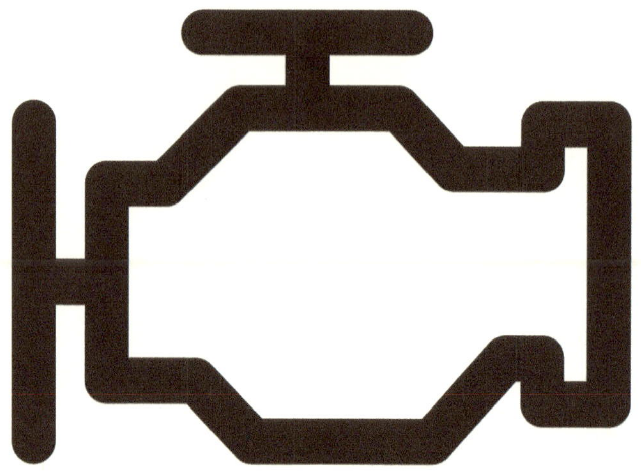

Hudson Motor Car Company of Detroit was the first manufacturer to incorporate these into their cars, doing so sometime in the 1930s.

Check Engine Light

Psalm 26:2 — Test me, Lord, and try me; examine my heart and mind.

Tune-Up 7

Psalm 27:14 - Wait for the Lord; be strong, and let your heart be courageous. Wait for the Lord.

One of life's greatest challenges and opportunities for growth comes when we are forced to delay gratification. We are not the best at waiting. When we have a need or a desire, our hearts often demand it right then and there. Frustration can quickly set in when we cannot simply press a button and get instant results. Diagnosing car problems can reveal our deep desire for immediate answers. Cars make certain sounds when operating normally, but when something changes, an odd noise or strange vibration, we know something isn't right. The cause of the problem may not be obvious right away. We have to wait, test, and observe before discovering what's wrong. Similarly, God uses these "waiting moments" in life to draw us closer. He invites us to pause, seek, and trust that He is at work even when we cannot see the full picture. Waiting on God is not simply about learning patience, it's about developing trust. He knows what we need and when we need it. If we will give Him time and space to work, He will guide, provide, and shape our hearts through the waiting.

In The Garage

Choose one of your situations to surrender to God's timing this week.

1. When have you struggled with waiting on God, and what did that experience reveal about your trust in His timing?

2. How might God be using your current "waiting season" to draw you closer to Him or to shape your character?

3. What practical step(s) can you take this week to replace frustration with prayer and trust when answers don't come quickly?

Lord, hear my voice when I call; be gracious to me and answer me.
Psalm 27:7

Tune-Up 8

Psalm 31:24 - Be strong, and let your heart be courageous, all you who put your hope in the Lord.

The psalmist ends his song with a declaration of hope. Though he has faced his share of distress, confidence in God has led him away from despair. Hope for the future now fills his vision because of God's character. God's very nature brings us confidence in both the good and the bad of life. We depend upon Him much like we depend on the tires of our car. The nature and reliability of those tires give us confidence that when we start out of the driveway, we'll arrive safely at our destination. In the same way, God's steadfast character gives us assurance for the journey ahead. Our hope for the future does not rest in our cleverness or in the resources of others on our behalf, but in the character of God. He has proven Himself loving, kind, and merciful toward us demonstrating His care through the sacrifice of Jesus Christ on the cross. When we place our faith in Him, hope is imparted to us. No matter where we may find ourselves in life, whether in seasons of joy or hardship, hope continues with us. Depend on God and trust that He will complete in you what He desires to bring about. In doing so, you will experience courageous hope.

In The Garage

Encourage someone who feels discouraged in their faith.

1. Where do you find it difficult to place full confidence in God's character? How can you entrust that area to Him?

2. When thinking about the "journey" you are on, how has God already proven Himself faithful, loving, and merciful in past seasons of distress?

3. What daily practices or reminders can nurture a courageous hope, one that depends not on circumstances, but on who God is?

Lord, I seek refuge in you; let me never be disgraced. Save me by your righteousness.
Psalm 31:1

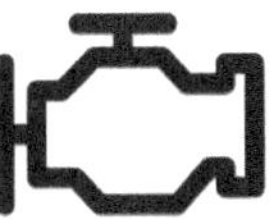

The Porsche 959 in 1986 was the first passenger car with TPMS, long before it became a U.S. mandate in 2000.

TPMS (Low Tire Pressure)

Psalm 121:3 — He will not allow your foot to slip; your Protector will not slumber.

Tune-Up 9

Psalm 29:2 - Ascribe to the Lord the glory due his name: worship the Lord in the splendor of his holiness.

The word "ascribe" isn't one we use often today. It means to assign or credit a quality to something. In Psalm 29:1–2, we're called to "ascribe to the Lord glory and strength." In worship, we are invited to do just that, to give God the credit, honor, and value He deserves. Worship offers us a chance to take the focus off ourselves and place it on the wonderful attributes of God. Worship can be like the headlights on our car. Headlights shine light forward, away from us, so that we can see the road ahead clearly. When they begin to dim, we replace them so we can continue to see well. In the same way, worship illuminates the greatness of God when we allow it to. It helps us see more clearly who He is, His power, His majesty, and His glory. As we worship, we lift our eyes from our own circumstances and catch a glimpse of the One who sits enthroned above all creation. God is worthy of our praise. When we take time to stop and look up, our hearts are reminded of His strength and splendor. Just as headlights are vital for driving safely, worship is vital for seeing the greatness of our Creator. Don't allow the light of your worship to grow dim. Keep it bright and focused, so that your heart remains fixed on the glory of God, the One to whom all honor and praise are due.

In The Garage

Spend 10 minutes today in worship without any requests.

1. What qualities or attributes of God do you need to "ascribe" to Him today in your worship and daily life?

2. How have you allowed the light of your worship to grow dim through distraction or routine?

3. In what ways does authentic worship help you shift focus from yourself to the greatness of God?

The Lord sits enthroned over the flood; the Lord sits enthroned, King Forever.
Psalm 29:10

Tune-Up 10

Psalm 34:1 - I will bless the Lord at all times; his praise will always be on my lips.

How does one keep life running smoothly? Psalm 34 gives us the answer. "I will bless the Lord at all times; his praise will always be on my lips." When we recognize God's goodness and acknowledge ourselves as the recipients of that goodness, we are transformed. Gratitude becomes the quality of heart that keeps every part of life working in harmony. As oil lubricates the motor in a car, so gratitude keeps us spiritually lubricated. It seeps into the deep recesses of our lives, protecting us from discouragement and distress. We may go through difficulties, but "the eyes of the Lord are on the righteous, and His ears are attentive to their cry" (v. 15). God is always there, watching over us. Our relationship with Him lifts our gaze upward instead of downward and inward. Just as we monitor the oil in our car, we must also monitor our gratitude. Oil must be changed and its level checked for best performance; likewise, gratitude must be refreshed and replenished as we meditate on God's goodness toward us. When we allow His care to become real in our daily lives, we "change our oil," so to speak, as we top off our gratitude for His love and faithfulness. "Taste and see that the Lord is good; blessed is the one who takes refuge in Him" (v. 8). May we never tire of being grateful for the goodness of the Lord.

In The Garage

Write a short list of daily blessings and thank God for them.

1. Where have you recently seen evidence of God's goodness in life, and how have you expressed gratitude for it?

2. What "maintenance" habits such as prayer, worship, or reflection keep your heart filled with gratitude instead of discouragement?

3. When challenges arise, how can you "lift my gaze upward" and renew your thankfulness for God's constant care?

The Lord is near the brokenhearted; he saves those crushed in spirit.
Psalm 34:18

Some dash lights can be noted and addressed at a later time, but not this light. Ignore this one and you may just be walking!

Engine Temperature / Overheating Light

Psalm 39:8 — Rescue me from all my transgressions; do not make me the taunt of fools.

Tune-Up 11

Psalm 40:3 - He put a new song in my mouth, a hymn of praise to our God. Mayn will see and fear, and they will trust in the Lord.

Times of praise lift us above our circumstances. When we walk through difficulties, remembering the moments when God moved in our lives enables us to praise Him even now. Praise rises from a heart full of gratitude for the Lord's presence. The psalmist reflected on God's many interventions. Because of that, trying times did not silence his praise. He looked back at what God had already done and found strength for what he faced in the present. Meditating on God's works smooths the rough places in our lives. It is like a well-tuned suspension on your car that allows you to travel over uneven roads without feeling every jolt. A functioning shock absorber softens what would otherwise be harsh. In the same way, when we reflect on how God has moved in our past, the difficulties that would normally disturb us are steadied. We begin to sense the comfort of our Lord. Take a moment and reflect on His moving in your life just as the psalmist did. Let the memory of God's involvement lift you above the rough travels this world brings. Offer Him praise as you rest in His faithful care.

In The Garage

Share with someone what God has recently done in your life.

1. What specific moment of God's past faithfulness can you recall, and how does remembering steady your heart right now?

2. Where are you feeling the "rough roads" of life the most, and how can you allow God's presence into those areas with praise instead of worry?

3. Reflect on God's past work in your life. Take a moment and praise Him for His work and presence in your life.

Let all who seek you rejoice and be glad in you; let those who love your salvation continually say, "The Lord is great!"
Psalm 40:16

Tune-Up 12

Psalm 42:1 - As a deer longs for flowing streams, so I long for you, God.

A wise disciple acknowledges the deep desires God has placed within their life. These desires find expression through longings that are woven throughout the human experience. We long for daily sustenance, meaningful relationships, shelter, and the assurance that we are spiritually connected to something greater than ourselves. Our cars have longings of their own. They are built with computers that monitor oxygen, fuel, exhaust, and electrical impulses. Each part must stay in harmony with the others for the car to operate at its best. In the same way, if we are to live at our best, our desires and longings must be in balance. The God-given desires we were created with are not meant to be ignored. They are meant to be embraced and brought into a healthy rhythm so we can live the life God intends for us. Many of us are careful to address our physical needs for food, shelter, and human connection. Yet the spiritual often receives far less of our attention. Psalm 42 speaks of a soul that thirsts for God as a deer pants for water. This longing is not vague or distant. It is real, urgent, and vital. Our spirits carry that same longing, whether we acknowledge it or not. Come to God and discover the balance and fullness only He can give to your life.

In The Garage

Set aside 10 quiet minutes each day to seek God's presence.

1. Which of your God-given longings receive most attention, and which ones do you tend to overlook or push aside?

2. When was the last time you sensed a real longing for God, and how did you respond to that inner thirst?

3. What steps can you take to bring your spiritual life into the same kind of balance and care you give to your physical and relational needs?

The Lord will send his faithful love by day; his song will be with me in the night, a prayer to the God of my life.
Psalm 42:8

Cars are starting to become caregivers. This light reminds us to buckle up for our safety.

Seat Belt Warning Light

Psalm 91:4 — He will cover you with his feathers; you will take refuge under his wings. His faithfulness will be a protetive shield.

Tune-Up 13

Psalm 32:5 - Then I acknowledged my sin to you and did not conceal my iniquity. I said, "I will confess my transgressions to the Lord," and you forgave the guilt of my sin.

David felt the heavy weight of guilt for his sins of adultery and murder. The sense of separation it created between him and God pressed hard on his heart. The joy of walking in fellowship with God was gone, but he knew the way back. He began by being brutally honest with God about his sin and the damage it had brought into his life. His heart and soul were wasting away inside, and he needed the refreshing and restoring touch of God. His honesty with himself and with God opened the way for him to experience God's forgiveness. Confession is simply agreeing with God about the truth of a matter. Once confession was made and forgiveness granted, David stepped into the freedom of a restored relationship. It is similar to how we feel when a broken car has finally been repaired. No matter how large or small the fix, that first drive makes the car feel new again. The stress of the malfunction is behind us, and everything is running as it should, filling us with relief and excitement. Having tasted God's forgiveness and restoration, David penned this wonderful psalm. We can know the same freedom before God when we acknowledge and confess our sin with a humble heart that seeks His forgiveness.

In The Garage

Confess one hidden sin in prayer and receive His cleansing grace.

1. Where do you sense the weight of unconfessed sin in your own life, and what would it look like to be completely honest with God about it today?

2. How have you experienced God's restoring touch in the past, and what does that remind you about His willingness to forgive now?

3. In what area of your walk with God do you need to seek the joy of restored fellowship, and what step of confession or surrender is He inviting you to take?

**How joyful is the one whose transgression is forgiven,
whose sin is covered!
Psalm 32:1**

Tune-Up 14

Psalm 38:21–22 - Lord, do not abandon me; my God, do not be far from me. Hurry to help me, my Lord, my salvation.

Even in the middle of our brokenness, God remains near. He forgives when we admit and confess our sin. The psalmist describes his wounds as boiling over with infection, a vivid picture of the inner damage caused by his own foolishness. Before he reached that condition, he ignored the signs that something was wrong. It is much like overlooking the warning lights on a car. The low oil light comes on, but instead of taking care of the issue, we brush it aside. In time the engine fails and the vehicle stops altogether. Those lights are not there to irritate us. They exist to protect us. In the same way, our lives give us clear signals when we drift into sin. Guilt, frustration, and a sense of distance from God all serve as indicators that something needs attention. The psalmist eventually paid attention to his warning lights. That honest recognition placed him in the right posture to ask for the mercy that God freely gives to the humble. Confidence grew in his heart as he turned to the Lord, knowing that He listens to those who come before Him in humility. Even with enemies pressing in, he trusted that God would forgive and deliver. Pay attention to your warning lights. Bring them to God with honesty, and allow Him to forgive, rebuild, and restore.

In The Garage

Journal how God has met you in times of weakness.

1. What warning signs from God have you been ignoring or explaining away?

2. In what area do you need to come before God with honest confession and humility, trusting Him to rebuild what is broken?

3. How can you respond today when you experience guilt, frustration, or distance from God so that those signals lead back to Him rather than farther away?

Lord, my every desire is in front of you; my sighing is not hidden from you.
Psalm 38:9

When this light comes on, better tend to it. Remember early drivers had to start their vehicles with a crank and the car lights were powered by gas. The horn of a car was a bell and indicators were powered by hand. I will replace my battery, thank you.

Battery / Charging System Warning

Psalm 84:5 — Happy are the people whose strength is in you, whose hearts are set on pilgrimage.

Tune-Up 15

*Psalm 51:10 - God, create a clean heart for me and renew a
steadfast spirit within me.*

The change that God brings into the disciple's life is a
lifelong process. We are not completely transformed on
the day of our salvation. Certainly, we are gifted the
indwelling of God the Holy Spirit, but sanctification takes
a lifetime. Our lives are filled with seeking God's will,
striving to integrate it, and maintaining what we have
learned. We vacillate between doing and not doing God's
will. The psalmist understood the necessity of cleansing
and renewal. Not that we lose our salvation, we do not,
but we grow weary of the doing and not doing. We need
times when God must renew us. Our cars and trucks need
the same kind of maintenance. Spark plugs wear out and
must be replaced to give the engine an optimal spark.
When the spark is right, the engine runs smoothly. When
God renews us, our lives run smoother. Habits are
refined, attitudes are godly, and our actions align with
Him. We run as we were designed to, efficiently and
rightly. Psalm 51 reminds us of this continual need:
"Create in me a clean heart, O God, and renew a right
spirit within me." Allow God to renew your heart afresh
and embrace the ongoing work of sanctification.

In The Garage

Invite the Holy Spirit to "spark" your heart, filling it with His guidance and strength for the week ahead.

1. In what areas are you vacillating between doing and not doing God's will, and how can you invite Him to restore consistency?

2. Like a car's spark plugs, what "worn-out" habits or attitudes need God's renewal so your life runs more smoothly?

3. Psalm 51 speaks of a clean heart and a right spirit. What is one practical step you can take today to cooperate with the Holy Spirit's ongoing work of sanctification?

Surely you desire integrity in the inner self, and you teach me wisdom deep within.
Psalm 51:6

Tune-Up 16

Psalm 20:7 - Some take pride in chariots, and others in horses, but we take pride in the name of the Lord our God.

We all have someone in our lives to depend on. Whether it is a spouse, a friend, a sibling, or our children, they are there when needs arise. Those are cherished as we know that no matter what comes our way we can depend on them for support. Having that kind of support system leads to a sense of security. We know we are not alone in this world. Though we trust in them, we must also realize our greater dependence on God. Consider our car's safety features. Air bags, brakes, and sensors are helpful, yet they can never replace our reliance on God. These earthly systems can fail and wear down with time. The psalmist reminds us that some place their trust in the things of this world, but he had placed his trust in God. God is our true source of security in this shifting world. He can be trusted and depended upon above all others in our lives. He will always be there when times of trouble come. All may fail us, but He will never fail. This is why we take pride in the name of the Lord our God.

In The Garage

Choose one area of life where you tend to rely on earthly security and place that trust in God instead.

1. In what situations do you find yourself depending on human support more than on God?

2. How has God shown Himself trustworthy in past moments of trouble or uncertainty?

3. What practical step can you take this week to deepen your daily reliance on God rather than on the things of this world?

May the Lord answer you in a day of trouble; may the name of Jacob's God protect you.
Psalm 20:1

This light strikes fear into drivers, especially those who tend to ignore the dash gauges. Generally, some say it is safe to drive 30–50 miles once the fuel light has illuminated, but who wants to chance it?

Low Fuel Light

Psalm 63:1 — God, you are my God; I eagerly seek you. I thirst for you; my body faints for you in a land that is dry, desolate, and without water.

Tune-Up 17

Psalm 37:3 - Trust in the Lord and do what is good; dwell in the land and live securely.

Being a passenger in a car can be an adventure, especially when the driver's ability is unknown. The passenger has to place complete trust in the person behind the wheel, not only to handle the car, but to follow the rules of the road and drive safely to the intended destination. The ride becomes far more enjoyable once the passenger realizes the driver knows what he or she is doing. Then the open fields and rolling hills in the background can be appreciated without worry. The psalmist calls us to trust the Lord in much the same way. We can place our full confidence in His guidance as we live out our days, knowing He handles the curves, the ups, the downs, and everything in between. God knows us because He is our Creator and we are His creation. We can trust Him to do what is right and fitting for us in every circumstance. As we learn to rest in that truth, we find the deep sense of security we have been longing for.

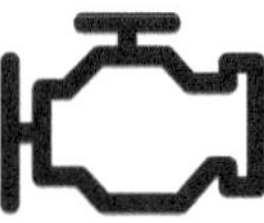

In The Garage

Write and pray a personal commitment to trust God completely.

1. Where in your life are you still trying to stay in the driver's seat rather than trusting God with the road ahead?

2. What "curves, ups, or downs" are you facing right now, and how can you invite God to guide you through them instead of carrying the weight alone?

3. How have you experienced God's steady hand or His care in the past, and how can remembering that help you rest more securely in Him today?

But the humble will inherit the land and will enjoy abundant prosperity.
Psalm 37:11

Tune-Up 18

Every car has the very same need. Each car or truck relies on an engine to provide the power that allows it to move. The engine supplies the strength that makes all the other parts work as they should. We are similar because we rely on God to be our source of life. The psalmist noted that God is our strength. From the beginning of creation, Scripture tells us that God formed Adam from the dust of the earth and then gave him breath and life (Genesis 2:7). No wonder the psalmist declares that God was his everything. All that we are is held together and supported by Him. He is our Creator and our God. We celebrate the life He has given us. Thanksgiving becomes a natural response when we recognize that He is not only God, but the One who made us and continues to sustain us. He is our God and we are His people. Place your trust in Him and celebrate His goodness toward us.

In The Garage

Memorize this verse and recall it in moments of worship.

1. In what areas of life are you trying to "run your own engine" instead of relying on God as a true source of strength?

2. How has God shown Himself to be Creator and Sustainer in recent weeks, and have you taken time to thank Him for it?

3. What is one heartfelt way you can express trust in God today and celebrate His goodness?

The Lord is the strength of his people; he is a stronghold of salvation for his anointed.
Psalm 28:8

Early brakes used simple levers to press a wooden block against the wheel.

Brake System Warning Light

Psalm 19:8 – The precepts of the Lord are right, making the heart glad; the command of the Lord is radiant, making the eyes light up.

Tune-Up 19

Psalm 119:105 - Your word is a lamp for my feet and a light on my path.

We tend to take our cars for granted. We hop in, turn a key or push a button, and off we go. That is, until the day the car stays silent when we expect the engine to roar to life. Those unexpected moments leave us standing there, a bit disoriented by the silence. What do we do then? We grab the repair manual and the OBD code reader. Those tools give us insight into the problem and point us toward a solution so the car can run again. Spiritually, we can feel just as disoriented by the circumstances of life. We may not have an OBD reader for our hearts, but we do have God's Word. He has given us wisdom, direction, and counsel in Scripture to show us what has gone wrong and how He intends to restore us. Through His Word, and with the help of the Holy Spirit, we can face what needs attention and let Him get us running again. The psalmist used the picture of light on a path, reminding us of how essential God's Word truly is. It is the light that helps us see where to step and how to move forward. It is our guide to real, lasting life.

In The Garage

Read a psalm today and note how it guides you.

1. When life feels silent or disorienting, where do you turn first for guidance, and what would it look like to turn to God's Word instead?

2. What "warning lights" might God be showing right now, and how is His Word inviting you to address them with honesty and trust?

3. In what area of life do you need to let Scripture and the Holy Spirit shine light on your next step so you can move forward with clarity?

I am resolved to obey your statutes to the very end.
Psalm 119:112

Tune-Up 20

Psalm 90:12 - Teach us to number our days carefully so that we may develop wisdom in our hearts.

A difference exists between knowledge and wisdom. Knowledge gives us information, but wisdom is the ability to apply that information. Responding to life in view of what we know and properly applying that knowledge is far more valuable. Life becomes manageable when the information we have leads to good decisions. It is much like the low fuel light on an automobile. When that light comes on and we acknowledge it, we immediately become intentional. Routes may be changed, the next fuel station noted, time is no longer wasted, and we become a more focused driver. The warning does not panic us, but it does direct us. Psalm 90:12 is like that low fuel light for us. Numbering our days is not meant to scare us. It is meant to nudge us toward being wise in how we live in light of God. He desires us to live with intentionality and purpose. We begin to live that way when we recognize the brevity of our lives. Priorities start to shift and distractions lose their pull as we learn to live for what carries eternal weight. Wisdom grows as we recognize life's brevity. Live each day with eternal purpose.

In The Garage

Set one spiritual goal for the next month.

1. Are you paying attention to the "low fuel lights" God is putting in front of you, or are you ignoring the signs that priorities need to shift?

2. Where do you need to become more intentional so you can live with the wisdom God desires?

3. What distractions might you need to lay aside to focus more clearly on what carries eternal purpose and weight?

Lord, you have been our refuge in every generation.
Psalm 90:1

High beams are great, but that extra light can be a help or a hindrance. Helpful on clear dark nights, but a hindrance in foggy situations.

High Beam Indicator

Psalm 27:1 — The Lord is my light and my salvation – whom should I fear? The Lord is the stronghold of my life – whom should I dread?

Tune-Up 21

Psalm 95:7 - For he is our God, and we are the people of his pasture, the sheep under his care.

Extended warranties on our cars are wonderful. The right warranty gives us a sense of security as we drive. We enjoy peace knowing that if our car or truck breaks down, help is available and the issue will be taken care of. Knowing we are in a right relationship with God brings a similar peace to our lives, though this peace is far greater and will never expire. The psalmist reflects on the relationship we can experience with God as a shepherd caring for His sheep. The sheep are looked after, and the problems they face are handled by the Good Shepherd, God the Father. We become part of God's flock when we come to Him through Jesus Christ. Just as we must sign up for the extended warranty on our car, we must enter God's Kingdom through Jesus Christ. When we do, His peace becomes ours, and we can declare with confidence, "I am under His care!"

In The Garage

Reflect upon the peace you have in God. Thank Him for making you part of His people.

1. What situation do you need to place under the care of the Good Shepherd instead of trying to manage alone?

2. Are you truly resting in the peace that comes from being in a right relationship with God, or are you still holding on to worry and fear?

3. In what practical way can you remind yourself this week that you belong to God's flock and that His care will never expire?

For the Lord is a great God, a great King above all gods.
Psalm 95:3

Tune-Up 22

Psalm 100:3 - Acknowledge that the Lord is God. He made us, and we are his — his people, the sheep of his pasture.

Ever wonder why the psalmist consistently calls us to acknowledge God? God is our Creator, and as such, He is the final authority on our identity and our purpose for being. We go to God to discover how our lives are to be lived and maintained. Just as you reference a car manufacturer when learning about your car or truck, the functions and features of your automobile have been determined by the one who made it. It only makes sense that you would go to their reference material to understand your car's features and maintenance schedules. In the same way, we go to the Word of God, The Bible, for an understanding of our features, functions, and purposes. He even has "maintenance" suggestions for us to keep us operating at our peak efficiency. And He directs us to Jesus for the clearest understanding of how we can live the life we were created to live.

In The Garage

Affirm your identity in Christ today.

1. Where are you relying on your own "manual" instead of going back to the Bible, provided by the One who designed you, and what might shift if you actually let God define your identity and purpose this week?

2. If your spiritual "maintenance schedule" reflects what you truly value, what habits or rhythms might the Father be inviting you to revisit, reset, or reintroduce in order to operate the way He intended?

3. As you look to Jesus, the perfect model of the life you were created to live, what specific feature or function of His character is God highlighting for you to imitate in a fresh way right now?

For The Lord is good, and his faithful love endures forever; his faithfulness, through all generations.
Psalm 100:5

The first windshield washer systems became available in the 1930's. Previously, drivers had to pull over and manually scrub their windshields with a mixture of water and soap.

Windshield Washer Fluid Low

Psalm 51:7 — Purify me with hyssop, and I will be clean; wash me, and I will be whiter than snow.

Tune-Up 23

Psalm 103:2 - My soul, bless the Lord, and do not forget all his benefits.

Remembering is an essential part of living. We remember our phone number, where we live, our family, our friends, and our co-workers. A good memory serves us well, but sometimes we need to be intentional in remembering. A log book of repairs to our car creates a confidence that we will not be left stranded on the side of the road. Knowing what repairs have been made and when the last tune-up was performed builds a steady sense of trust. In the same way, taking inventory of how God has blessed us strengthens our trust in Him and fills our hearts with gratitude. When we intentionally remember God's goodness, our worship becomes deeper and more genuine. Knowing that He has been good to us encourages our own faithfulness toward Him. We can join the psalmist who chose to remember what God had done and allowed those memories to shape his life. As we recall God's benefits, our hearts are lifted, our trust is renewed, and our steps grow steadier on the road ahead.

In The Garage

Write a short prayer of thanks for God's mercy.

1. What specific blessings or "repairs" has God made in your life that you need to intentionally remember today?

2. How might keeping your own kind of spiritual log book help build a deeper trust in God and guard your heart from forgetting His goodness?

3. In what ways can recalling God's past faithfulness shape the way you worship and walk with Him this week?

As a father has compassion on his children, so the Lord has compassion on those who fear him.
Psalm 103:13

Tune-Up 24

Psalm 89:1 - I will sing about the Lord's faithful love forever; I will proclaim your faithfulness to all generations with my mouth.

Car guys and gals can be a strange lot. Loyalty to a specific manufacturer can almost border on the insane. One may love Toyotas while another is sold on Fords. They will only own that particular brand and will joke with each other about how their car is the best. The banter can get very vocal and loud. Does your loyalty to Jesus get the same amount of energy and excitement? The psalmist declared that he would forever sing God's praises. If our cars call for such public display, our love for God calls for even more effort on our part to let the world around us know of our devotion to Him. Jesus has paid a tremendous sin debt on our behalf. We should be shouting from the housetops our love and devotion to Him. Others should know that we are grateful to God for salvation and that they can join us in His Kingdom. We want our friends to drive our brand of car. Should we not care even more about their eternal destination?

In The Garage

Take a few minutes today to intentionally speak a word of gratitude about Jesus to someone you meet.

1. How do you pour energy into showing a love for Jesus as you do into the things you get excited about every day?

2. If the psalmist was willing to sing God's praises forever, what is holding you back from speaking openly about His goodness?

3. If you care enough to recommend a car brand to someone, how can you point them toward the Savior who has secured their eternal destination?

They rejoice in your name all day long, and they are exalted by your righteousness. Psalm 89:16

Your parking brake is a multi-tool. It is a tool to keep your car or truck from rolling away once parked, but it doubles as an emergency brake in the event of a primary brake system failure.

Parking Brake Engaged

Psalm 46:10 — Stop your fighting, and know that I am God, exalted among the nations, exalted on the earth.

Tune-Up 25

Psalm 67:1 - May God be gracious to us and bless us; may he make his face shine upon us.

Imagine driving down a rural highway at night. With no streetlights, the darkness makes it difficult to see, and every mile feels uncertain. Then you switch on your headlights. Even better, you flip on the brights. Suddenly the road opens up in front of you. What was hidden a moment ago becomes clear, and traveling forward becomes safer and far more confident. That is what God offers us. The psalmist in Psalm 67 cries out for the blessing of God's illumination. Life is dangerous when we try to navigate it in the darkness of sin, stubbornness, or resisting God's leading. But that is not the only option available to us. We can choose to live in the light of God's will and commands. When we make the decision to follow Him, He lights the road we are called to travel just as surely as bright headlights cut through the night. God's shining face is His gracious guidance. His revelation shows us how to live, where to walk, and how to reflect Him in the world. Our part is to trust Him to light the way and to rely on the blessing of His presence as He shines on us.

In The Garage

Take a few quiet minutes today to ask God where He wants to shine His light in your life, then act on the first step He shows you.

1. Where are you trying to navigate life in your own dim light instead of trusting God to shine the way forward?

2. What specific step of obedience is God illuminating for you right now, and are you willing to walk in it?

3. How can you let God's light, in you, guide others who may still be trying to find their way in the dark?

Let the nations rejoice and shout for joy, for you judge the peoples with fairness and lead the nations on earth.
Psalm 67:4

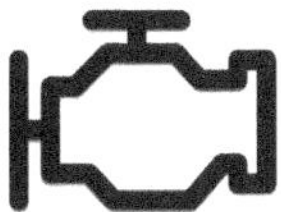

Tune-Up 26

Psalm 71:18 - Even while I am old and gray, God, do not abandon me, while I proclaim your power to another generation, your strength to all who are to come.

We grow old. This fact can never be changed, challenged, or corrected. While many fight this reality, the disciple of God will embrace growing old and seek to pass on their faith in Jesus Christ. Time wisely spent will lead to the next generation taking up the disciple's journey in Christ. You can position your life in such a way that your so-called old fashioned faith becomes a new reality in the lives of those coming up behind you. It is very similar to why we maintain and care for our cars. Our goal is to have our cars last as long as possible so that the next generation can enjoy them as we have. The features once considered new are now old. New owners often find those features interesting and engaging. Our faith, though considered old, still holds a certain fascination for those who discover that God is still saving people from their sins. We can embrace growing old as we share with the next generation a vibrant and exhilarating faith that they can live and pass on.

In The Garage

Share a testimony with someone younger in faith

1. How are you embracing the reality of growing old in a way that helps you pass on your faith in Jesus Christ?

2. In what ways can your so-called old fashioned faith become a new reality for someone coming up behind you?

3. What can you do to share a vibrant and exhilarating faith with the next generation?

***My lips will shout for joy when I sing praise to you
because you have redeemed me.
Psalm 71:23***

Not only does cruise control help moderate the temperature of your engine, it also helps with fuel economy. Some studies have found that you can save up to 10% on your gas budget every year simply by using cruise control.

Cruise Control Indicator

Psalm 37:23 — A person's steps are established by the Lord, and he takes pleasure in his way.

Tune-Up 27

Psalm 73:28 - But as for me, God's presence is my good. I have made the Lord God my refuge, so I can tell about all you do.

Trusting in God for a lifetime is at times difficult. We cannot always see what is ahead of us. Pain, despair, and suffering often hinder us from seeing what lies before us, and though these seasons are limited in duration, they can still weigh heavily on our hearts. When we cannot see a clear or pleasant future, it is easy to grow despondent. We tend to view life by looking backward instead of forward. We want to trust God with our lives because that is what we have learned of Him from His Word. Yet present circumstances can jade our outlook and make faith feel harder than it should be. God can be trusted just as a driver must be trusted to navigate the road. As a passenger, our view may be through fogged up glass, rain pelted glass, or even a glass so dirty that nothing ahead seems clear. The temptation is to doubt the driver, yet if we are to arrive safely, we must trust the skill and knowledge of the one behind the wheel. The driver knows the automobile and its abilities far better than we do. Trust God when things are not what we desire and allow Him to guide us through. His vision is clear even when ours is not, and He will lead us safely to where we need to be.

In The Garage

Choose one area of your life that feels unclear or discouraging and intentionally turn it over to God in prayer, asking Him to guide you through it as your trusted driver.

1. Where are you looking backward instead of trusting God with what lies ahead?

2. How has your present circumstances been jading your outlook and weakening your confidence in God's leading?

3. What would it look like today to trust God as fully as a passenger trusts the driver who sees the road more clearly?

Who do I have in heaven but you? And I desire nothing on earth but you. Psalm 73:25

Tune-Up 28

Psalm 80:7 - Restore us, God of Armies; make your face shine on us, so that we may be saved.

Ever wish you had a restart on a project or relationship? The desire for renewing is common. We see the wrongs we have done and the consequences that follow. We may even try to correct those wrongs. At times we see small improvements, but more often we make matters worse. Our own abilities at restoration fall short. Our intentions may be sincere, but we simply do not have the capacity to restore what truly needs repairing. This is especially true in our relationship with God. His grace reaches toward us and changes us through the forgiveness He provides in Jesus Christ, His Son. Think of a skilled car restorer working on a faded and dull finish. Over time, paint loses its luster, and no amount of casual effort will bring back its shine. But a trained restorer uses the right tools, techniques, and knowledge to renew the surface to a beautiful, glossy finish. Yet even this comparison falls short, because while the restorer repairs what is seen, God goes deeper. His restoration does not stop at the surface. He transforms the heart, so the shine comes not only from the outside, but from within. As Psalm 80:7 pleads, "Restore us, O God Almighty; make your face shine upon us, that we may be saved." Let God restore you today.

In The Garage

Invite God to examine the areas of your life that have grown dull and ask Him to begin His restoring work there.

1. Where do you recognize the consequences of your own attempts at self-restoration, and how might you surrender those areas to God's care?

2. In what ways have you seen God renew what you could not fix on your own?

3. What part of your heart needs His transforming shine today?

Then we will not turn away from you; revive us, and we will call on your name.
Psalm 80:19

The 1980's saw the addition of the "Door Ajar" light to the dashboard. Some automakers went a step further and had their cars speak to you saying that your, "Door is ajar!".

Door Ajar

Psalm 141:3 — Lord, set up a guard for my mouth; keep watch at the door of my lips.

Tune-Up 29

Psalm 61:2 - I call to you from the ends of the earth when my heart is without strength. Lead me to a rock that is high above me.

One of the common fears of traveling is being stranded with car trouble. Before a long trip, we check and double-check our vehicles to ensure a safe journey. Trouble cannot be predicted, yet we can prepare and have a plan for whatever may come. Many people pay a yearly fee to AAA as insurance for the possibility of a flat tire or a dead battery far from home. No matter where they find themselves, they have confidence that help is close at hand. The psalmist reminds us that God's people have an even greater help available. God is always present for those who call on Him. When we bow in prayer, we receive strength that helps us navigate the difficult moments of life. God responds to the needs of those who seek Him. Knowing that He watches over us gives peace, joy, love, and most of all hope. We can live securely because our God loves us and never stops keeping His eyes on us.

In The Garage

Write a prayer expressing your dependence on God.

1. In what areas of your life do you tend to rely on your own preparation, and how can you bring those concerns before God in prayer?

2. When have you recently experienced God's nearness in a moment when you felt overwhelmed, and what did that teach you about His care?

3. How can the assurance of God's constant watchfulness shape the way you respond to uncertainty in the days ahead?

I will dwell in your tent forever and take refuge under the shelter of your wings.
Psalm 61:4

Tune-Up 30

Our desire should be for the righteousness of God in the world. We should have a strong inward conviction that calls for an honest appraisal of who we are on the inside. The psalmist calls for God to establish His righteousness upon the earth. His appeal for such vivid action demonstrates just how committed he is to seeing evil suppressed and God's righteousness rule. He begins by asking pointed questions that guide us to examine our hearts and motives, ensuring that we are not acting with injustice toward our fellow mankind. In the same way, a car must track straight in order to travel safely down the road. To ensure this, questions must be asked of the alignment of its wheels. The vehicle is placed on a rack, and its alignment is carefully examined against a fixed standard. Likewise, the psalmist's opening questions place our hearts on the rack. They compel us to measure our lives against God's standards, not our own, to ensure that we are living in righteousness both inwardly and outwardly. Do we desire God's righteousness to dwell upon the earth as the psalmist did?

In The Garage

Meditate on your own desire for God's righteousness to be established on the earth.

1. Where might your heart be out of alignment with God's standards, even if your outward actions appear acceptable?

2. How does your life reflect being comfortable with injustice when it does not affect you personally?

3. What specific attitudes, words, or actions does God need to correct so that your life tracks straight according to His righteousness?

Then people will say, "Yes, there is a reward for the righteous! There is a God who judges on earth!" Psalm 58:11

According to the National Highway Traffic Safety Administration, frontal air bags have saved more than 50,000 lives over a 30-year period.

Air Bag

Psalm 91:11 — For he will give his angels orders concerning you, to protect you in all your ways.

Tune-Up 31

Psalm 92:5 - How magnificent are your works, Lord, how profound your thoughts!

Delight is a word that seems seldom used. We may substitute other words, yet this one carries a depth of emotion we need to recapture. To delight in something reflects deep appreciation and awe for the object of our attention. As disciples of Jesus Christ, our worship should be marked by delight. The psalmist speaks of his deep appreciation and meditation on the wonderful works of God. God is seen in His creation, and the psalmist stands in delight before Him. He considers the greatness of God's works and the depth of His thoughts, and his heart responds in worship. We, even more than the psalmist, should delight in our God. Our worship ought to rise higher and loftier than that of old, for we have come to know God's salvation. Modern people understand delight well. One may delight in the body style of a certain automobile—the curve of the fenders, the richness of its color, the beauty of the interior panels. All these draw out admiration and pleasure from the observer. In much the same way, we should allow the sacrifice of Jesus, the grace of the Father, and the indwelling presence of the Holy Spirit to draw out our delight. Meditate on God and learn to delight.

In The Garage

Meditate on God and list your top 5 reasons to delight in Him.

1. What works of God most readily draw out your delight, and how often do you pause to meditate upon them?

2. In what ways has your worship become familiar or routine rather than rising from awe and appreciation?

3. How does the sacrifice of Jesus, the grace of the Father, and the indwelling of the Holy Spirit shape the depth of your delight in God?

**It is good to give thanks to the Lord, to sing praise to
your name Most High,
Psalm 92:1**

Tune-Up 32

Psalm 117:2 - For His faithful love to us is great; the Lord's faithfulness endures forever. Hallelujah!

One enduring trait we long for in our cars and trucks is longevity. We boast that our vehicle has outlasted other makes and models. Comparisons are made, and stories of miles traveled are told for years. Accolades given to our cars become part of our lives, and though some of those vehicles are no longer with us, the memory of their faithful service lives on. Though God cannot be compared to our cars or trucks, His faithfulness in our lives similarly fuels our praise and testimony. God is to be praised because He has outlasted every security this world offers. While the systems of the world rise and fall, God's grace and mercy have stood the test of time. From the garden until now, God has been faithful to every generation. Psalm 117 calls all people to praise the Lord because His steadfast love is great and His faithfulness endures forever. We can sing of His love because it surpasses all that this world has ever offered or ever will offer. The next time you find yourself praising your car or truck, pause for a moment and reflect on the greater reason you have to praise God. Instead of lifting up what serves for a season, lift up the One whose love and faithfulness endure forever.

In The Garage

*Thank God for His enduring faithfulness whenever you are tempted
to boast in something that will not last.*

1. What temporary securities in life do you speak highly
of, and how often do your words reflect praise for God's
enduring faithfulness instead?

2. In what ways have you personally witnessed God's
grace and mercy remain steady while the systems or
supports of this world have changed or failed?

3. How can you more intentionally lift up God in daily
conversations and testimonies, rather than focusing on
the things that have only served you for a season?

**Praise the Lord, all nations! Glorify him, all peoples!
Psalm 117:1**

Imagine driving your car without this invention. This common feature may be one of the most taken for granted features on your car.

Front and Rear Defrost

Psalm 36:9 — For the wellspring of life is with you. By means of your light we see light.

Tune-Up 33

Psalm 85:9 - His salvation is very near those who fear him, so that glory may dwell in our land.

God's people long for His presence. When sin divides and we feel the distance created by a lifestyle of disobedience, restoration is found through repentance and confession. Psalm 85 reflects the joy that follows a restored relationship with the Lord. After a season of wandering, sensing His nearness again brings a deep and unmistakable joy to the heart. Often, we do not fully understand the severity of our time away from God until the Holy Spirit moves freely in us once more. It is similar to putting new tires on a car. The first drive reveals just how poor the ride had become on the worn ones. The improved handling, tracking, and smoothness create a new appreciation for the vehicle we thought we already knew. In the same way, forgiveness for our waywardness toward God renews our awareness of His nearness. We begin to recognize how empty, cold, and harsh life had become when we were pushing Him away through disobedience. Restoration opens our eyes to what had slowly been lost. May we draw near again and cry out with the psalmist, "Faithful love and truth will join together; righteousness and peace will embrace" (Psalm 85:10).

In The Garage

Examine your heart, confess any areas of disobedience, and draw near to the Lord in repentance, trusting Him to restore the joy of His presence.

1. Where have you grown distant from God through subtle or ongoing disobedience that you have tolerated?

2. How has your spiritual life felt empty, cold, or strained, and what might that reveal about a need for restoration?

3. What step(s) can you take to walk in obedience and remain attentive to the nearness of the Lord?

Righteousness will go before him to prepare the way for his steps.
Psalm 85:13

Tune-Up 34

Psalm 120:1 - In my distress I called to the Lord, and he answered me.

The heart of a disciple is beautifully reflected in the psalmist's words. He cries out to the Lord for help as he seeks strength and guidance while navigating turbulent times. The circumstances surrounding him are difficult and unsettling, yet his first response is to turn to God. We understand the psalmist because the world in which we live also leaves us desiring God's help and strength. We face seasons that seek to influence us toward what is evil rather than good. Our hearts need a fresh move of God in order to have the strength to make wise, good, and righteous choices. God willingly directs our steps as we surrender to His guidance. Modern cars are often equipped with screens that provide directions to our destination, but only if we are willing to follow what is shown. We input the destination and trust the guidance that leads us there. In the same way, through prayer and petition, we come before God and ask Him for wisdom. James reminds us in James 1:5 that when we ask, God willingly gives wisdom so that we can make righteous choices. The wisdom the psalmist sought in his distress is the same wisdom available to us today. When we are willing to seek God and obey His direction, He faithfully leads us along the path that honors Him.

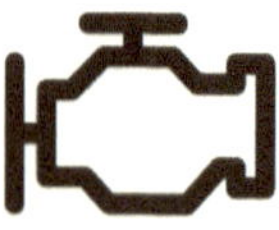

In The Garage

Commit to seeking God daily through prayer and surrender, trusting His guidance to lead you toward wise and righteous choices.

1. What influences are trying to lure you away from God's wisdom and toward what is not good?

2. How are you pursuing God's guidance when you face difficult or unsettling circumstances?

3. What step(s) of obedience is God asking you to take as you trust Him to direct your path?

Lord, rescue me from lying lips and a deceitful tongue.
Psalm 120:2

Tune-Up 35

Psalm 119:8 - I will keep your statutes; never abandon me.

How does one actually tune up one's life? What is the process? To begin, we must recognize that there are tools available for the job. The greatest tool at our disposal for getting our lives running right again is God's commands. His commands guide us to life, but only if we are willing to move beyond mere knowledge. Knowing what God expects of His people is simply knowledge. Wisdom, however, is the application of that knowledge. Wisdom is lived out when we actually obey God and keep His commands. The idea is similar to replacing a car battery. When the battery dies, the car no longer works. After diagnosing the problem, we must follow proper procedures for removal and replacement to avoid damaging the vehicle's electrical system. Ignoring the steps or taking shortcuts only creates more problems. In the same way, God's way of living comes with clear steps. We must obey them to avoid causing further damage to our lives. Obedience is not optional maintenance but necessary repair. As we carefully follow the repair procedures for our cars, let us also faithfully follow God's commands for living. In doing so, we allow Him to restore what is broken and keep our lives running as they were designed to run.

In The Garage

Identify a command of God you already know but have not been obeying, and make an effort to obey it.

1. What commands of God do you clearly know but have treated as information rather than instruction?

2. Where have you have ignored God's steps and created further damage as a result?

3. What would faithful obedience look like in your life if you trusted that God's way truly leads to life?

I will praise you with an upright heart when I learn your righteous judgments.
Psalm 119:7

Other Titles in the
"Coffee With The Preacher Series"

Coffee With The Preacher: A Devotional Companion As You Walk Through The Gospel of John

Coffee With The Preacher: A Devotional/Journal For The Book Of Romans

Brewed with Fire and Faith: Daily Reflections from the Early Church

Closing Remarks

Thank you for allowing me to share my thoughts as we have "tuned up" our lives together. As we come to the end of these devotionals, my prayer for you is that you have been drawn closer to Jesus Christ and that your heart delights in the Lord and His Word. Return to these devotions and remember the lessons God has revealed to you. Do not allow these lessons to remain within the pages of this book; allow them to dwell within you, guide your steps, shape how you live, and bring praise to God through a life transformed. Once again, thank you for joining me on this "Tune-Up," and may God richly bless you through His Son, Jesus Christ.

ALL FOR CHRIST!

Dr. Raymond Grabert

Author Bio

Dr. Raymond Grabert has been a pastor for over 30 years. Currently, he serves as pastor of Big Ridge Baptist Church, D'Iberville, MS. His native state is Louisiana, where he met and married his wife of 36 years. Educated at New Orleans Baptist Theological Seminary, he holds the B.G.S, M.DIV., and D.MIN. Degrees.

www.ingramcontent.com/pod-product-compliance
Lightning Source LLC
Chambersburg PA
CBHW062229150726
47991CB00006B/2503